ELECTRIC ANIMALS

ELECTRIC CATFISH MAKE ELECTRICITY!

BY LOUIS MALLORY

Please visit our website, www.garethstevens.com. For a free color catalog of all our high-quality books, call toll free 1-800-542-2595 or fax 1-877-542-2596.

Cataloging-in-Publication Data
Names: Mallory, Louis.
Title: Electric catfish make electricity! / Louis Mallory.
Description: New York : Gareth Stevens Publishing, 2024. | Series: Electric animals | Includes glossary and index.
Identifiers: ISBN 9781538292907 (pbk.) | ISBN 9781538292914 (library bound) | ISBN 9781538292921 (ebook)
Subjects: LCSH: Catfishes–Juvenile literature. | Electric fishes–Juvenile literature.
Classification: LCC QL637.9.S5 M355 2024 | DDC 597'.49–dc23

Published in 2024 by
Gareth Stevens Publishing
2544 Clinton Street
Buffalo, NY 14224

Copyright © 2024 Gareth Stevens Publishing

Designer: Claire Wrazin
Editor: Natalie Humphrey

Photo credits: Cover, pp. 1, 15 BLUR LIFE 1975/Shutterstock.com; background (series art) Romashka2/Shutterstock.com; p. 5 Juniors Bildarchiv GmbH/Alamy Stock Photo; p. 7 Pavaphon Supanantananont/Shutterstock.com; p. 9 File:Electric_Catfish_electric_organ.svg/Wikimedia Commons; pp 11, 17 James Emery/flickr; p. 13 Mark Conlin/Alamy Stock Photo; p. 19 Artorn Thongtukit/Shutterstock.com; p. 21 File:Malapterurus sp. in Gifu World Fresh Water Aquarium.jpg/Wikimedia Commons.

All rights reserved. No part of this book may be reproduced in any form without permission in writing from the publisher, except by a reviewer.

Printed in the United States of America

CPSIA compliance information: Batch #CW24GS: For further information contact Gareth Stevens, New York, New York at 1-800-542-2595.

CONTENTS

One Shocking Catfish 4
Spotting a Catfish 6
An Electric Layer 8
How Many Volts? 10
Hunting at Night 12
Hungry Catfish 14
Stay Away! 16
Communication 18
Pet Electric Catfish 20
Glossary 22
For More Information 23
Index 24

Boldface words appear in the glossary.

One Shocking Catfish

There are many different species, or types, of catfish found around the world. But some catfish have a special skill: they can make **electricity**! The electric catfish is a species of catfish that can make a strong electrical charge.

Spotting a Catfish

You can find electric catfish in many of Africa's **freshwater** rivers and lakes. They have gray or brown bodies. Unlike most fish, they don't have **scales**. Instead, they have thick skin. Electric catfish are usually around 4 feet (1 m) long.

An Electric Layer

To make electricity, electric catfish have a jellylike **layer** under their skin. This layer is made of special **muscle** cells that cover the catfish's whole body. The cells make different amounts of electricity that the catfish can use to hunt or keep itself safe.

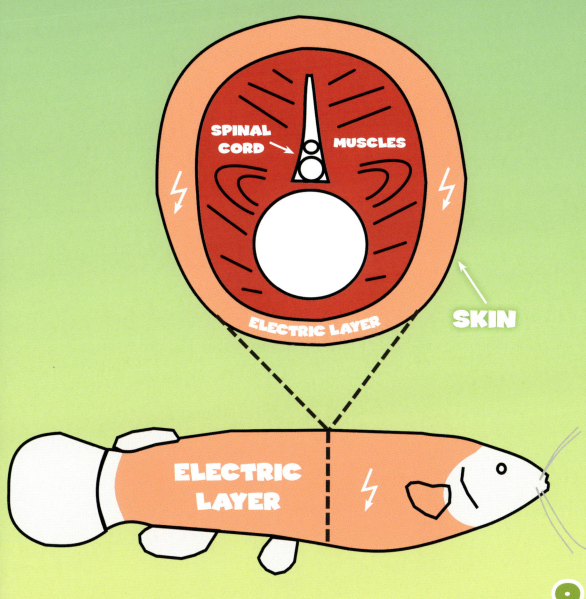

How Many Volts?

How strong is an electric catfish's charge? Scientists measure electrical **energy** in volts. Electric catfish can make around 450 volts of electricity. That's enough of a shock to stun an animal. "Stun" means the animal is unable to move or think clearly.

Hunting at Night

Electric catfish hunt at night. Because they can't see very well, electric catfish use electricity to find their meal. They use small electrical **pulses** to sense when food is nearby. When their meal gets close enough, electric catfish eat it whole!

Hungry Catfish

Electric catfish are **carnivores**. They like to eat bugs, eggs, and other fish. Catfish can eat food that's nearly half as big as they are! After eating, electric catfish won't need to eat again for a few days.

Stay Away!

Electric catfish are territorial. This means they try to keep other catfish and animals away from the area they think belongs to them. When an animal comes into an electric catfish's territory, the catfish uses its electricity to stun them or scare them away!

Communication

Electric catfish use their electricity to **communicate** with other electric catfish. They are usually telling other electric catfish to back off! If another catfish doesn't leave their territory, the electric catfish will fight!

Pet Electric Catfish

Some people keep electric catfish as pets. They need big **tanks**. Their shocks won't kill a human, but they might hurt. Electric catfish are usually kept alone. With the right care, electric catfish can live for around 10 years as pets!

GLOSSARY

carnivore: An animal that eats meat.

communicate: To share thoughts or feelings by sound, movement, or writing.

electricity: A kind of energy that flows and is made by the movements of animals.

energy: Power used to do work.

freshwater: Water that is not salty.

layer: One thickness of something lying over or under another.

muscle: One of the parts of the body that allow movement.

pulse: Short increases in electricity.

scale: One of the flat plates that cover a fish's body.

tank: A large container for storing things.

FOR MORE INFORMATION

BOOKS

Krekelberg, Alyssa. *Essential Fish*. Minneapolis, MN: Abdo Publishing, 2022.

Temple, Colton. *Amazing Animal Electricity*. Minneapolis, MN: Kaleidoscope, 2022.

WEBSITES

Electric Catfish Fish Facts—AZ Animals
www.a-z-animals.com/animals/electric-catfish/
Learn more fun facts about electric catfish.

Electric Catfish
www.britannica.com/animal/electric-catfish
Check out more interesting facts about electric catfish.

Publisher's note to educators and parents: Our editors have carefully reviewed these websites to ensure that they are suitable for students. Many websites change frequently, however, and we cannot guarantee that a site's future contents will continue to meet our high standards of quality and educational value. Be advised that students should be closely supervised whenever they access the internet.

INDEX

Africa, 6

cells, 8

communication, 18

food, 12, 14

hunting, 8, 12

lake, 6

muscle, 8

pet, 20

river, 6

scales, 6

skin, 6, 8

territory, 16, 18

volts, 10